Shake It, Morena!

AND OTHER FOLKLORE FROM PUERTO RICO

compiled by
Carmen T. Bernier-Grand

illustrated by Lulu Delacre

The Millbrook Press • Brookfield, Connecticut

To the youngest generation in my family: Matthew, JR, Clara, Itzel, Emilians, Marcos segundo, Werther Guillermo, and Xiomara Salome. — C.B-G

Para Ana-Mita — L.D.

Text copyright © 2002 by Carmen T. Bernier-Grand
Illustrations copyright © 2002 by Lulu Delacre

Library of Congress Cataloging-in-Publication Data

Shake it, morena! : and other folklore from Puerto Rico / compiled by Carmen T. Bernier-Grand;
illustrations by Lulu Delacre.
     p. cm.
Summary: An illustrated collection of games, songs, traditions, and stories from Puerto Rico.
English and Spanish.
ISBN 0-7613-1910-7 (lib. bdg.)
 1. Folklore—Puerto Rico—Juvenile literature. 2. Children –Folklore. 3. Puerto Rico—Social life and customs
—Juvenile literature. [1. Folklore—Puerto Rico. 2. Spanish-language materials—Bilingual.] I. Bernier-Grand,
Carmen T. II. Delacre, Lulu, ill.

GR 121.P8 S53 2002
398'.097295—dc21 2001032945

Published by
The Millbrook Press, Inc.
2 Old New Milford Road
Brookfield, Connecticut 06804
www.millbrookpress.com

Book design by Tania Garcia
Printed in Hong Kong
5 4 3 2 1

Acknowledgements
Thanks to those who always believed in this book: Harold Underdown, Jennie Dunham,
Dominic Barth, and Jean Reynolds.
Mil gracias también a La Plinita Mayor, Nilda Villanueva de Morales, y a su compañera
de Parkville School, Magda Ramos.

Author's Note

Everybody has a culture, and we learn the most about that culture as a child. We don't have culture lessons. It's just that from the time we wake up in the morning until we go to bed at night, we experience bits and pieces of our culture – while we're eating, while at school, and especially while we're having fun. For what is culture if it isn't stories, games, holidays, food, music, crafts, traditions, religion, language?

Shake It, Morena! is a potpourri of songs, riddles, and stories I heard and games I played as a child in Puerto Rico. It covers activities from awakening in the morning, to learning at school, to coming home, to being with the family and then going to bed.

This book is an opportunity to play alongside the children of Puerto Rico, and learn a bit about their culture.

It is my hope that educators can use this book to teach Spanish, math (Dos y Dos Son Cuatro), natural science (Puedo o No Puedo), social studies (Playground Passport), reading (The Legend of the Hummingbird), writing (Spelling Game), physical education (Shake It, Morena!).

¡Diviértansen! (That's how we say "Have fun!" in Puerto Rico!)   — CTB-G

Artist's Note

I want to share with you my own game that I played when I was young. Growing up in Puerto Rico I loved to look at, play with, and chase the many kinds of lizards that roamed around. I was especially fond of the tiny brown ones that seemed to be everywhere. When I was about five years old, I was really good at catching them by their tails, gently opening their mouths, and then attaching them to my earlobes. I would wear them as earrings until the tiny brown lizards got tired of hanging, and dropped to the ground in search of less thrilling experiences.

Now they are way too fast for me to catch, so I paint them and leave them for you to find. There are twenty-seven lizards hidden in the pages of *Shake it, Morena!* Have fun finding them!
—LD

Contents

Waking Up Song

The music for this song is on page 44.

The parents sing:

Levántensen soldados	Get up, you soldiers.
que las siete son,	Seven o'clock is ringing,
y ahí viene el sargento	And here comes the sergeant,
con su batallón.	Marching and singing.

The sleepy children answer:

Déjalos que vengan.	Let them all come.
Déjalos venir.	Hear them at the door.
Véte para la porra,	Just leave us alone.
y déjanos dormir.	Can't you hear us snore?

Children in Puerto Rico also wake up with the crow of roosters and with the song of the reinitas, little birds with yellow chests.

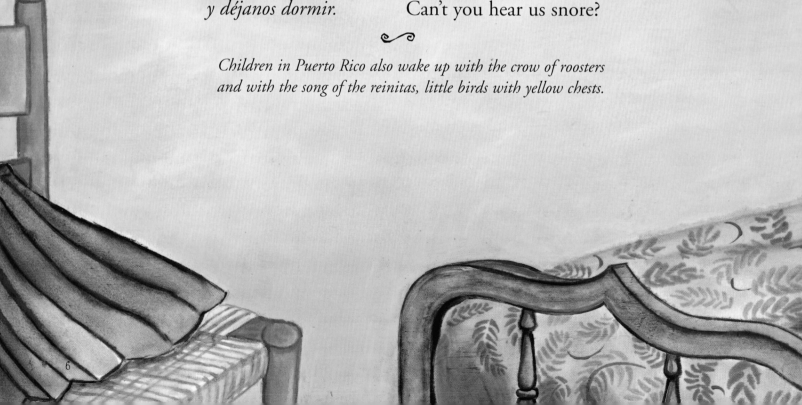

Jeringonza Secret Language

Jeringonza is a secret language. To tell secrets in jeringonza, add "chi" before each syllable of a word, like this:

Chime chivoy chia
chico chimer
chila chima chillor chica
chide chiPe chipe.
(Me voy a comer
la mallorca de Pepe.)

ChiI Chiam chigo chiing
chito chieat
chiPe chipe's
chisweet chiroll.
(I am going to eat
Pepe's sweet roll.)

A language similar to jeringonza is Pig Latin. But in Pig Latin you take off the first letter of the word, put it at the end, and add to it "ay." For example, "hello" would be "ellohay."

Café Game Song

The music for this song is on page 44.

*Yo te daré, te daré,
  niña hermosa,
Te daré una cosa, una
  cosa que yo sólo sé.
¡Café!
Con A:
Ya ta dará, ta dará,
  naña harmasa,
Ta dará ana casa, ana
  casa qua ya sala sá.
¡Cafá!*

I'd give you, I'd give
  you, pretty girl,
I'd give you something
  only I know.
Coffee!
With A:
A'd gava yaa, A'd, gava,
  pratta garl
A'd gava yaa samathang
  A anla knaw.
Caffaa!

Sing it with the other vowels: E, I, O, U.

La Calle Ancha Game

La calle ancha is a a clapping game similar to Miss Mary Mack.
To play it, face your partner and sing:

La calle an-cha-cha-cha   The wide street
[Clap your hands together three times when you say cha-cha.]

de San Bernar-do-do-do   of Saint Bernard
[Clap your hands three times against your
   partner's hands when you say do-do.]

tiene una fuen-te-te-te   has a fountain
[Slap your hips three times.]

de cuatro ca-ños-ños-ños.   with four pipes.
[Slap your thighs three times.]

Los cuatro ca-ños-ños-ños   The four pipes
[Clap your right hand against your partner's right hand three times.]

dan agua dul-ce-ce-ce   have sweet water
[Clap your left hand against your partner's left hand three times.]

Para que to-men-men-men   for the Andalusians
[Clap both your hands against your partner's hands three times.]

los andalu-ces-ces-ces.   to drink.
[Clap your hands three times.]

❧

*La Calle Ancha as well as other Puerto Rican games have Spanish roots
because Puerto Rico was a colony of Spain for over 400 years.
In 1898, however, Spain gave Puerto Rico to the United States.*

Shake It, Morena!

The music for this song is on page 45.

Choose a leader who stands at the center of a circle.
Everybody sings, claps, and dances, shaking their hips, to the rhythm of:

Chequi morena, chequi.	Shake it, *morena*, shake it.
Chequi morena che	Shake it, *morena*, eh!
¿A dónde está ese ritmo?	Where is that rhythm?
¡Caramba!	Caramba!
Del merecumbé. ¡Eh!	Of *merecumbé*! Eh!
Un pasito adelante	A little step forward
Un pasito atrás	A little step back
Y dando la vuelta,	And turn around
Dando la vuelta	Turn around
¿Quién se quedará?	Who will be It?

When the leader hears "*dando la vuelta,*" he closes his eyes and
turns in a circle, pointing at the players. When the song ends, he stops.
The player he is pointing at becomes the new leader.

In "Shake It, Morena!" we can trace three of the main influences in Puerto Rico.
We see the African influence in the rhythm of the *merecumbé* and the person of
the *morena*, a brown-skinned woman; the Spanish influence in its language; and
the American influence in the English words. But since there's no "sh" sound
in Spanish, most Puerto Rican children say, "*chequi*" instead of "shake it."

*Puerto Ricans love to dance. They think that a party without dancing
is not a party. People of all ages are invited to most parties.
And everybody dances, from the baby to great-grandfather.*

Mi Escuelita School Song

The music for this song is on page 47.

Mi escuelita, mi escuelita,
yo la quiero con amor,
Porque en ella, porque en ella,
es donde aprendo mi lección.
Por la mañana muy temprano,
lo primero que yo hago
es saludar a mi maestra
y después a mi trabajo.

My little school, my little school,
I love it so dearly,
Because in it, because in it,
I learn my lessons.
Early in the morning,
I come in and then
I greet my teacher and
pull out my book and pen.

Most students in Puerto Rico wear uniforms to school.
This is true for public as well as private schools.

Math Riddles

Dos vieron caer un mangó;
diez lo recogieron
y treinta y dos lo comieron.
(Dos ojos; diez dedos;
y treinta y dos dientes)

Two saw a mango falling;
ten picked it up;
and thirty-two ate it.
(Two eyes; ten fingers;
and thirty-two teeth.)

Mangoes in Puerto Rico are so juicy that
sometimes it's better to eat them in the bathtub!

El boticario y su hija,
el doctor y su esposa,
se comieron nueve huevos,
y les tocaron tres.
(La hija del boticario es
  la esposa del doctor.)

The pharmacist and his daughter,
the doctor and his wife,
ate nine eggs,
and they had three each.
(The pharmacist's daughter
  is the doctor's wife.)

Discutían dos marineros
sobre el dinero que tenían.
Uno de ellos dijo:

—Si tú me das un centavo,
tendría el doble que tú.

—Eso no sería justo—
dijo el otro.

—Es mejor que tú
me des un centavo
y entonces tendríamos lo mismo—.

¿Cuánto tenía cada uno?
(Uno tenía cinco centavos
y el otro tenía siete centavos.)

Two sailors were arguing
about the money they had.
One of them said:

"If you give me a penny,
I'd have twice the money you have."

"That won't be fair,"
the other one said.

"It's better for you to give me a penny,
and we will have the same amount."

How much money did each one have?
(One of them had five cents
and the other had seven cents.)

Another name for centavos, pennies, in Puerto Rico is chavos.
But in Mexico, chavos means "boys."

People in Puerto Rico use the same money used in the United States.

16

Dos y Dos Son Cuatro Song

The music for this song is on page 46.

Dos y dos son cuatro
cuatro y dos son seis,
seis y dos son ocho
y ocho, dieciséis.
Y ocho veinticuatro
y ocho treintaidós.
Más diez que le sumo,
son cuarentaidós.

Two and two are four
four and two are six,
six and two are eight
and eight, sixteen.
And eight more is twenty-four
and eight thirty-two.
If I add ten more,
then I have forty-two.

Choosing a Game Leader

When Puerto Ricans want to know who the leader is, they ask:

¿Quién se queda?   Who stays?

And instead of saying, "You're IT!" They say:

Te quedas.   You stay.

To choose *quien-se-queda*, they use a rhyme similar to eenie, meenie, minie, moe, in which they point to each player, saying:

De tín marín de los pingué   Of *tín marín* of the *pingués*
cúcara mácara títere fue.   *cúcara, mácara,* puppet is.

The last player pointed at is *quien-se-queda*.

Puedo o No Puedo Game

Choose a player to be Mamá. Mamá stands far apart from the other players, who stand on a starting line. Mamá chooses a player, an animal, and the number of steps for the player to take. For example, Mamá may say:

Da dos pasos de ratóncito.   Take two mouse steps.

The player must say:

¿Mamá, puedo o no puedo?   Mother, may I or may I not?

If the player moves without saying *"Puedo o no puedo,"* he or she loses a turn. But if the player remembers, Mamá answers:

Puedes.   You may.

The player takes the mouse steps. The game continues with Mamá calling other children to take any number of other animal steps. The animals might be:

cabra	goat
hormiga	ant
caballo	horse
gallo	rooster
perro	dog

The first child who gets close enough to tag Mamá becomes the new mother.

"Puedo or no puedo" resembles "Mother May I."

STORYTIME:
The Legend of the Hummingbird

In 1493, when the Spaniards landed in Puerto Rico, the Tainos (also referred to as Arawak) lived in Boriquén, their name for the island. They were a peacable tribe whose only enemies were the Caribs, who came from other islands to steal Taino women.

The story below tells the story of a Carib in love with a Taina. There are other books that tell this folktale: Once In Puerto Rico *by famous folklorist and author Pura Belpré and* The Legend of the Hummingbird *by Michael Rose Ramírez, who heard the story from her grandmother, Carmen Bautista Millán Soto. Both stories use the traditional names of Alida for the Taina and Taroo for the Carib. The story retold here uses the indigenous word Ris, which according to Luis Henández Aquino's* Diccionario de Voces Indígenas de Puerto Rico *means red, and it uses Guarcariga, the indigenous word for hummingbird.*

Ris, the daughter of a Taino Indian chief, resting her feet in the warm spring, noticed a face reflected in the water. Slowly, she turned around and looked behind her. First, she saw two strong legs with cotton bands below the knees. Ris looked up, her heart pounding, for the Taino did not wear such bands. This young man standing before her had very long hair, like that of a fierce Carib! Her people kept their hair short.

Ris stood up, ready to run, but the man gently held her arm.

"Do not be afraid!" he said. "I come in peace."

Ris peered at him, surprised that he could speak her language and wondering if he was telling the truth.

"My name is Guacariga, and yes, I am a Carib."

Ris pulled her arm from his hand and began to run toward the bushes, for she knew the Caribs liked to steal Taino women.

"Do not go," Guacariga cried, running after her. "I'm not going to take you. Please, listen to me."

His gentle voice made Ris stop. She looked into his black eyes.

"The first time I came here to fight your people," he said, "I saw you!"

"Me?"

"Yes, you were right here by the spring. After that, I vowed not to fight anymore. I have come here every day hoping to tell you, and today I found you."

Guacariga spoke while looking straight into Ris's eyes. She listened to him, knowing that he was telling the truth.

"My mother is a Taino woman. My father, a Carib, stole my mother from here a long time ago."

Ris stepped back.

"Do not fear," Guacariga said. "I will never steal a woman."

Ris sighed.

Guacariga continued: "I learned from my mother to be a man of peace, but my father wants me to be a warrior."

"Did you learn my language from your mother?" Ris asked.

"Yes, she speaks it to me."

Day after day Ris and Guacariga saw each other, and soon they became friends. Then their friendship turned into love. But their meetings by the warm spring were always brief. Ris knew her father would be angry to discover she had a Carib friend. Yet as careful as she was, one day Mayey, a Taino man who wanted to marry Ris, saw her with Guacariga. Mayey ran to the village and told Ris's father.

When Ris returned home, her father scolded her. "You are forbidden to go to the warm spring, and you are to be married to Mayey before the moon is full."

Ris tried to tell her father that Guacariga was not like the other Caribs, but her father did not believe a Carib could be good. "You will not marry a Carib," he said.

Ris tried to run to the warm spring to tell Guacariga. But her father held her by her arm, took her inside her hut, and didn't let her go out.

That evening, Ris cried out to her god. "Ay, Yukiyú, help me! Do what you will with me, but do not let me marry Mayey."

Yukiyú took pity on her and changed her into a delicate red flower.

The next day, and every day after, Guacariga waited for Ris by the warm spring. Sometimes he stayed there until the sky filled with stars.

One evening, the moon took pity on him. "Guacariga," the moon called. "Wait no longer for Ris. Your secret was revealed, and Ris's father was going to marry her to Mayey. In her grief, she called on Yukiyú. He heard her plea and changed her into a red flower."

"Ay," cried Guacariga. "What is the name of the flower?"

"Only Yukiyú knows," the moon replied.

Guacariga called out, "Ay, Yukiyú, help me find Ris!"

Yukiyú listened to Guacariga, as he had listened to Ris, and changed him into a tiny, brilliant blue-green bird.

"Fly, Guacariga," Yukiyú said, "and find your love among the flowers."

Off went Guacariga, flying swiftly. As he flew, his wings made a humming sound.

Ever since, Guacariga has flown from flower to flower, kissing every red flower with his long, slender bill—hoping to find Ris. But he has not found her yet. And so, to this day, he flies, from flower, to flower, to flower . . .

Animal Riddles

Canto en la orilla;
vivo en el agua;
no soy pez,
ni tampoco cigarra.
(La rana.)

I sing by the river bank;
I live in the water;
I'm not a fish;
I'm not a grasshopper.
(The frog.)

¿Qué es? ¿Qué es
del tamaño de una nuez,
sube la cuesta y no tiene pies?
(El caracol.)

What is it? What is
the size of a nut,
climbs the hill, and has no feet?
(The snail.)

Sometimes in the flower stands in Puerto Rico there are many snails.

Hablo pero no pienso;
lloro pero no siento;
río sin razón;
y miento sin intención.
(Una cotorra.)

I speak but I don't think;
I cry but I don't feel;
I laugh without a reason;
and I lie without intention.
(A parrot.)

The Puerto Rican parrot is approaching extinction and is now
found only in the Puerto Rican rain forest of El Yunque.

Es tan grande mi fortuna
que estreno todos los años
un vestido sin costura
de colores salpicado.
(La culebra.)

My fortune is so large
that every year I wear
a new dress of splashy colors
made without a stitch.
(The snake.)

En lo alto vive;
en lo alto mora;
en lo alto teje;
la tejedora.
(La araña.)

High she lives;
high she dwells;
high she weaves;
the weaver.
(The spider.)

Playground Passport Game

Make flags of different countries (or states) and signs with the names of those countries. Place sign and flag in the playground, each country apart from the others. Choose a leader. Assign to the rest of the players a country, and ask them to stand by the flag of the country assigned. The leader, who doesn't have a country, teases the other players saying several times:

Yo quiero un pasaporte	I want a passport.

Then the leader says:

Yo quiero un pasaporte *para ir a*	I want a passport to go to

He or she says a country and runs to it. At this point, everybody changes countries. The person without a country is now the leader.

If you are in the United States, you won't need a passport to go to Puerto Rico because the island is a territory of the United States. Puerto Ricans are U.S. citizens, so they have American passports.

Another Puerto Rican version of Pasaporte *is "Por aquí hay candela," in which the leader asks the others if they have candlelight.*

Riddles on the Way Home

¿Puedes brincar más alto que
una pared de doce pies?

(Sí, porque la pared
no puede brincar.)

Can you jump higher than
a twelve-foot-high wall?

(Yes, because a wall
cannot jump.)

The Spaniards built a tall, thick wall in San Juan, the capital of Puerto Rico.
They did that to protect the city from its enemies, especially pirates.

¿Por qué las gallinas ponen huevos?
(Porque si los tiran, se rompen.)

Why do hens lay eggs?
(Because if they throw them,
the eggs break.)

¿Con qué se puede llenar un saco *para que pese menos?* *(Con agujeros.)*	With what can you fill a bag so it weighs less? (With holes.)
¿Qué es lo primero que hacemos *cuando despertamos?* *(Abrir los ojos.)*	What is the first thing we do when we wake up? (Open our eyes.)
¿Qué es que si se habla se rompe? *(El silencio.)*	What can break just by speaking? (Silence.)

Everything breaks the silence in Puerto Rico. In the country, the tree frog called coquí *and the rooster sing loud enough to keep everybody awake. In the towns, the street vendors loudly announce their wares—fruit, bread, brooms. In the cities, the honk of cars makes a lot of noise. And everywhere there is music!*

Snacks

Limbers

Pour pineapple (piña) juice into ice trays.
Keep the trays in the freezer until the juice hardens.
Put the limber cubes in cupcake cups and eat them!

The flavorful ice cubes were called limbers after Charles Augustus Lindbergh visited Puerto Rico in 1928. Lindbergh was the first person to fly alone across the Atlantic from New York to Paris, France. Because he was already a celebrity when he visited Puerto Rico, he was invited to participate in a carnival parade. But Lindbergh didn't accept the invitation. Then he was asked if he would present a flower bouquet to the Queen of the parade. He accepted, but instead of handing it to her, he threw it. Puerto Ricans found Lindbergh so cold that they called the ice cubes they were beginning to make in their new refrigerators "lindberghs." Soon, the word changed to "limbers," which sounds more like Spanish. Limbers are made year around because it's always hot in Puerto Rico.

Chupón De China

Tear a small door at the top of an orange.
Open the little door, and bring it to your mouth.
Squeeze the orange, and suck out its juice.

"Chupón" means sucking, so *chupón de china* means "sucking orange."

In most Spanish-speaking countries oranges are "naranjas." In Puerto Rico, however, though the word naranja *is understood, most oranges are called "chinas." This is because some of the flavorful Puerto Rican oranges grow on trees that came from China.*

Esconde la Prenda Guessing Game

Ask all the players to sit. Choose three to five players, and ask them to
stand in front of the others with their hands behind them.
Take a pebble and go behind the standing players, closing their hands and saying:

Esconde la prenda	Hide the gem
Escondela bien	Hide it well
Que no te la vea	So no prince
Ni el hijo del rey	Can foretell.

Put the pebble in the hand of one of the standing players, but keep going as
if you have not given the pebble to anyone yet. Say the rhyme two or three
more times, then ask the standing players to stretch out their hands out with
their fists tightly closed. The sitting players have to guess who has the pebble
and in which hand. The person who guesses right is the next leader.

If the players are not too young, the leader may tease
them once by keeping the pebble to himself.

*Because it is so warm in Puerto Rico, people gather outside
their homes to chat with their neighbors while
their children play* Esconde la Prenda *and other games.*

Caracol Game

Draw a snail shell on a concrete surface and divide it into squares. The object of the game is to hop into each square, beginning at the outside square, getting to the center (home), and hopping back out without touching the lines. The player may rest both feet at home. A player who completes the course throws a pebbble to the shell. The player writes his or her name on the square where the pebble falls. If the square already has a name, the player chooses the next available square. That player is the owner of that square, and he or she may rest on it. All the other players have to hop over it. The game ends when it gets to be impossible to hop over so many squares. The person with his or her name on the most squares wins.

Caracol means snail shell. Although the name of the game is in Spanish, Puerto Rican children have always called the center of the shell "home."

Spelling Game

Choose a leader. The other players stand behind a
starting line, and the leader stands far away from the line.

The leader says:

¡Telegrama!   Telegram!

The other players say:

¿Para quién?   For whom?

The leader chooses a player, who asks:

¿Qué dice?   What does it say?

The leader says a word. The player takes a step for each letter in
the word while saying the letter. If the player misspells the word, he
or she must return to the starting line. The first player who gets
close enough to tag the leader becomes the new leader.

*Telegrams are short messages sent by telegraph, a system that can transmit
rapidly by encoding the text. But people in Puerto Rico and
in many parts of the world seldom send telegrams anymore.
Now it is more convenient to phone, or to send a fax or e-mail.*

Dinnertime Riddles

Fui al pueblo,
compré de ellas;
vine a mi casa
y lloré con ellas.
(Cebollas.)

I went to town,
and I bought them;
I came home,
and I cried with them.
(Onions.)

Una cajita chiquita
blanca como la sal,
todos la pueden abrir,
pero nadie la puede cerrar.
(El huevo.)

A small box
white like salt,
anybody can open it,
but nobody can close it.
(The egg.)

Subo siempre llena
y bajo siempre vacía;
si no me apresuro,
la sopa se enfría.
(La cuchara.)

I always go up full,
I always come down empty;
if I don't hurry,
the soup gets cold.
(The spoon.)

Cien damas en un castillo,
y todas visten de amarillo.
(El arból de chinas.)

One hundred ladies in a castle,
all dressed in yellow.
(An orange tree.)

Tell Me a Story: Teaser

Había una vez y dos son tres
un gato con las patas al revés.
¿Quieres que te lo cuente otra vez?

Once upon a time
there was a cat with upside-down legs.
Do you want me to tell you the story again?

This teaser is repeated many times, then the storyteller tells a real story.

Tell Me a Story: Juan Bobo

Juan Bobo was playing in his shack, when he saw a *jíbaro,* a man from the countryside, by the door.

"*¿Qué quiere?*" Juan Bobo asked him. "What do you want?"

"Water," the *jíbaro* said. "Please."

Juan Bobo went to the kitchen and brought out a pitcher of *maví,* a Puerto Rican drink made with bark. He served a glass to the *jíbaro.*

"*Este maví está rico,*" the *jíbaro* said. "It's delicious."

"*¿Quiere más?*" Juan Bobo asked him. "Would you like more?"

"*Sí.*"

Juan Bobo filled up the glass, and the *jíbaro* said, "*Gracias.* This *maví* is really good."

"*¿Quiere más?*" Juan Bobo asked, when he saw that the *jíbaro's* glass was empty.

"*Mira,*" the *jíbaro* said. "Look, your mother might get angry at you if you give me more."

"*No se preocupe,*" Juan Bobo answered. "Don't worry. She's not here."

"*Está bien.* Give me another sip."

Juan Bobo filled his glass, and the *jíbaro* drank it.

"*¡Caramba!*" the *jíbaro* said. "That was good."

"Don't you want this last little bit?" Juan Bobo asked him.

"*No, muchacho, gracias,*" the *jíbaro* said on his way out. "God bless you, and I hope your mother doesn't get angry at you for this."

"*¡Qué va!*" Juan Bobo said. "She didn't want that *maví* anymore. A mouse fell in it last night. And this morning, we took it out dead."

Tooth Fairy Rhyme

Ratoncito, ratoncito,
te doy este dientito,
para que me dejes unos chavitos.

Little mouse, little mouse,
I give you this little tooth,
So you'll leave me a few cents.

The tooth fairy in Puerto Rico is a mouse called Ratoncito Pérez.

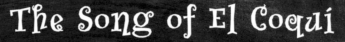

The Song of El Coquí

The music for this song is on page 48.

El coquí, el coquí
a mí me encanta
es tan lindo el cantar del coquí.
Por las noches al ir a acostarme,
me adormece cantándome así:
Coquí, coquí,
Coqui-qui-qui-quí;
Coquí, coquí,
Coqui-qui-qui-quí.

The kokee, the kokee
enchants me,
It is so beautiful, the kokee's song.
At night when I'm going to bed,
it makes me sleepy singing:
Kokee, Kokee,
Kokee-kee-kee-KEE;
Kokee, Kokee,
Kokee-kee-kee-KEE.

A coquí is a tiny tree frog with huge eyes. It sings all night! When
you first go to Puerto Rico, it is very hard to fall asleep because of
the singing of el coquí. *But when you return to the United States,*
it is hard to go to sleep without the song of el coquí.

Waking Up

G

Le - ván-ten-sen sol - da - dos, que las sie-te son, y a-hí vie-ne el sar - gen - to con su ba-ta-

llón. Dé-ja-los que ven - gan, Dé-ja-los ve - nir, Vé-te pa-ra Eu - ro-pa, y dé-ja-nos dor - mir.

D7   **G**

Cafe

Amin   **E7**   **Amin**   **A7**   **Dmin**

Yo te da - ré, _____ te da - ré, ni - ña her - mo - sa. Te da-

G7   **C**   **Dmin**   **Amin**   **E7**   **Amin**

ré u - na co - sa. _____ u - na co - sa que ya so - lo sé. !Ca - fé!

44

Shake It, Morena

D

Che-qui mo-re - na, che - qui. Che-qui Mo-re - na che. ¿A-

A7

dón - de es - tá ę - se rit-mo? ¡Ca-ram - ba! del me - re-cum - bé? ¡Eh!

D   A7

Un pa - si - to ą - lan - te, Un pa - si to ą trás. Y

D   A7

dan-do la vuel-ta, Dan-do la vuel - ta ¿Quién se que-da - ra?

D

45

La Calle Ancha

La ca - lle an - cha - cha - cha de San Ber - nar - do, do,
Los cua - tro ca - ños - ños - ños dan a - gua dul - ce - ce -

do, tie - ne u - na fuen - te - te - te, con cua - tro ca - ños, ños, ños.
ce Pa - ra que to - men - men - men los an - da - lu - ces - ces ces.

Dos y Dos

Dos y dos son cua - tro, cua - tro y dos son seis,
Y o - cho vein - ti - cua - tro y o - cho trein - ta j - dós

seis y dos son o - cho y o - cho, diez - i - séis.
más diez que le su - mo, son cua - ren - ta j - dós.

46

Mi Escuelita

Mi es-cuel - i - ta, me es-cuel - i - ta, yo la quie-ro con a-

mor, Por-que en e - lla, por-que en e - lla es don-de a-pren-do mi lec-

ción. Por la ma-ña - na muy tem - pra - no, lo pri-me-ro que yo

Fine

ha - go es sa-lu-dar a mi maes-tra, y des-pués a mi tra - ba - jo.

D. C. al Fine

47

El Coquí

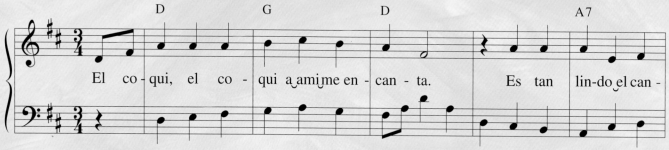

El co-quí, el co-qui a ami me en - can - ta. Es tan lin-do el can -

tar del co - qui._____ Por las no-ches al ir a-cos - tar-me

me a-dor me-ce can - tan-do a - si._____ Co - qui, co -

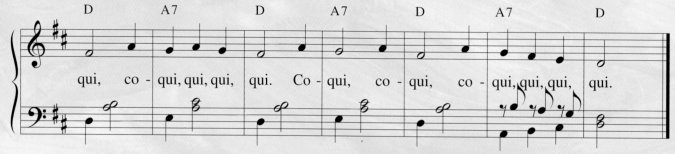

qui, co - qui, qui, qui, qui. Co - qui, co - qui, co - qui, qui, qui, qui.